Dewitt, Lynda

AUTHOR

Eagles, Hawks, & Other Birds of

TITLE                              Prey

22404                        Jnf 598.91

| DATE LOANED | BORROWER'S NAME | DATE RETURNED |
|---|---|---|

22404                              Jnf 598.91

# EAGLES, HAWKS, AND OTHER BIRDS OF PREY

# EAGLES, HAWKS, AND OTHER BIRDS OF PREY

## LYNDA DEWITT

FRANKLIN WATTS A FIRST BOOK 1989
NEW YORK LONDON TORONTO SYDNEY

Illustrations by Anne Canevari Green
Cover photograph courtesy of: Animals/Animals (John Pontier)

Photographs courtesy of: Aperture Photobank & Alaska Photo: pp. 3 (Joel Bennett), 8 (bottom, R. Van Nostrand), 15 (Tom Bean), 21 (Nancy Simmerman), 36 (Tim Fitzharris), 58 (top, Joel Bennett); Photo Researchers: pp. 8 (top, Leonard Lee Rue, III), 29 (Ken M. Highfill), 33 (Alan Carey), 45 (Tom McHugh), 56 (Jeff Lepore); Peter Arnold: pp. 14 (Robert Villani), 42 (Stephen J. Krasemann); Bruce Coleman: 37 (Leonard Lee Rue, III), 43 (Kevin Byron), 46 (F.J. Alsop, III), 52 (Kenneth W. Fink), 55 (Gary Meszuros); Animals/Animals: pp. 17 (top, M. Amsterman), 22 (Leonard Lee Rue, III), 24 (Zig Leszczynski), 34 (Joe & Carol McDonald), 50 (C.C. Cockwood); Zoological Society of San Diego: p. 17 (bottom); Academy of Natural Sciences, Philadelphia, © R. Bierregaard/VIREO: p. 28; Lynda DeWitt: p. 58 (bottom).

Library of Congress Cataloging-in-Publication Data
DeWitt, Lynda.
Eagles, hawks, and other birds of prey / Lynda DeWitt.
p.    cm. — (A First book)
Bibliography: p.
Includes index.
Summary: Discusses birds of prey, what makes them different from other birds, and how to observe them. Also describes the physical characteristics, habits, and natural environment of various species of vultures, eagles, kites, hawks, falcons, and owls.
ISBN 0-531-10570-9
1. Birds of prey — Juvenile literature.    [1. Birds of prey.]
I. Title.    II. Series.
QL696.F3D48    1989
598'.91 — dc19                                        88-31371    CIP    AC

# CONTENTS

THANKS TO DRS. MARK FULLER,
JOHN WESKE, SCOTT WARD, AND
JIM RODGERS.

# EAGLES, HAWKS, AND OTHER BIRDS OF PREY

TWO BIRDS OF PREY, AN
OSPREY (ABOVE) AND
A RED-TAILED HAWK
(BELOW), IN FLIGHT

# CHAPTER ONE

## BIRDS OF PREY

### POWERFUL, WILD, AND FREE

With its outstretched wings, a large bird catches rising columns of warm air. It rides the surging air currents like a surfer rides the waves. Its eyes, set on the ground hundreds of feet below, focus on a sudden movement in the grass.

Immediately, the bird thrusts its head out and down, pumps its wings, and dives. As the bird falls, its eyes narrow into slits, and its wings close in tight against its body. This living dive-bomber, a peregrine falcon, clenches its feet and within seconds strikes its target—a smaller bird, or perhaps a mouse. The falcon severs the animal's spine with its bill before carrying it away.

Peregrine falcons are birds of prey, or *raptors*. Like eagles and hawks, they have strong feet, razor-sharp claws, or *talons*, and a hooked bill. The birds use these body parts like weapons to strike, stab, and rip prey. They kill not for fun or sport, but to survive. They are part of a natural food chain in which one organism gets energy by eating another organism. Mature birds of prey are at the top of their food chain. They have few, if any, natural predators.

But they do have enemies. Pollution, particularly from pesticides, has wiped out thousands of birds, bringing several species close to extinction. And in North America each year, forests, marshes, and other *habitat* areas where raptors hunt and breed are destroyed for development. Over the years, federal and state governments have protected large tracts of land against development. These parks, forests, and refuges provide places for raptors and other wildlife to hunt and breed. The need to preserve wilderness areas extends to Central and South America, where many birds of prey spend the winter.

Knowing where birds of prey live, what they eat, and how they behave will help us protect them. By preserving habitats and curbing pollution, people can further ensure a place on earth for these magnificent animals.

You can learn a lot about birds just by watching them. All you need are binoculars, a bird field guide, and patience. You also may want paper and a pencil to jot down what birds you see and when and where you see them. You may even decide to start a "Life List" of all the birds you identify.

head — eye
nape — bill
— nostril
— shoulder
back —
— breast
— belly
feathers —
— leg
— talon
tail —

detail of a foot with talons

ANNE CANEVARI GREEN

You can watch birds at many different places—parks, ponds, streams, marshes, fields, cemeteries, and back roads. You may see more action around dawn and dusk, particularly with owls. And remember, do not disturb the birds or their habitats. Try not to scare parent birds away from their nest, and never steal nests or eggs.

# CHAPTER TWO

## VULTURES

### PREYERS OF DEAD FLESH

An old, sick deer lies dying in the woods. Soon after the deer takes its last breath, a dark bird appears in the distant sky. Another one soon joins it. Before long, nine or ten birds are circling overhead. They soar lower and lower until they glide to a stop near the deer carcass. The deer's life is over, but its body will supply these birds with the food and energy they need to live.

Jostling for position around the dead deer, the birds grunt, hiss, and leap at one another. Blood covers them as they rip open the carcass with their hooked bills and plunge their heads inside. One of the birds bends over and pecks out the deer's eyes, swallowing them whole.

These large, dark birds are vultures. They do not kill for food like other birds of prey. Their talons are too small and weak for that. Instead, they feed on the meat, or *carrion*, of dead animals. Like garbage collectors, vultures get rid of waste that would otherwise decay and spread disease.

**BLACK VULTURES**

Vultures often fly more than 100
miles (160 km) a day—over woods,
farms, highways, garbage dumps, and piers
—in search of food. They don't get the least bit sick
from diets that would kill most other animals. This is
because powerful enzymes in the stomach destroy
harmful bacteria. Vultures even use their food to defend
themselves. When frightened, they don't scratch or claw
—they vomit. After a day of scavenging, vultures may
bathe in shallow pools or streams. The head is feather-
erless, making clean up easy. After they bathe, they
rest, or *roost,* in trees and clean and smooth out their
feathers with their bills, a behavior known as *preening.*

Vultures store some of the food they eat in a pouch, called a *crop,* located on the side of the throat half-way between the mouth and stomach. By gradually releasing food into the stomach, the crop maintains the steady flow of food needed to sustain these big birds. Vultures weigh so much after a big meal that they have to hop awkwardly along the ground and may have trouble taking off. But once in the air, they fly gracefully for hours on outstretched wings.

**A TURKEY VULTURE**

Three kinds of vultures live in North America: the turkey vulture, the black vulture, and the California condor. Turkey vultures range across much of the United States and Canada. You may see one soaring above a field or highway. Up close, its bald, red head will remind you of a turkey's, which is how it got its name. If you live in the southeastern region of the United States, you may see black vultures; these black-headed birds often live near towns and cities. With a bright orange head and a *wingspan* the length of a small car, the California condor is unmistakable. But, you cannot see one in the wild. For now, all of the California condors in the world live in either the San Diego Zoo or the Los Angeles Zoo.

Like all birds, vultures lay eggs. But, unlike most birds, they don't build a nest. They simply lay their eggs on a cliff shelf, in a shallow cave, or in a hollow tree. Turkey vultures and black vultures usually lay two eggs each year, while California condors lay just one egg every other year. They skip a year because their young from the previous year still depend on them.

Incubation lasts about a month for turkey vultures and black vultures and about two months for condors. The newly-hatched young, or *nestlings*, are fed regurgitated food from their parents' crops. At about two months of age, the young turkey and black vultures

AN ADULT
CALIFORNIA
CONDOR

A KEEPER AT THE SAN DIEGO ZOO
FEEDS THE BABY CONDOR MOLLOKO.

*fledge,* or take their first flight. Condors fledge when they are six months old. Turkey and black vultures have adult feathering, or *plumage,* by their second autumn, and they mate and rear young of their own the following spring. Condors do not have adult plumage until their fifth year, and mating does not begin until they are six or seven years old.

The condors' slow maturation makes it difficult for them to recover from population losses. By 1985, after years of decline due to pesticide and lead poisoning, power line collisions, and a shrinking habitat, only six known California condors remained in the wild. All lived in the Los Padres National Forest in southern California. Scientists decided to capture the birds and add them to the captive populations at the San Diego and Los Angeles zoos.

On April 29, 1988, a baby condor hatched at the San Diego Zoo, becoming the twenty-eighth existing California condor. It was the first one bred in captivity. The bird was named *Molloko,* the Indian word for condor. As more captive birds mature and breed, some may be released to the wild one day.

# CHAPTER THREE

## EAGLES

### FIERCE YET FRAGILE

The bald eagle with its striking white-feathered head, dark brown body feathers, and huge yellow bill was chosen nearly two hundred years ago to represent the United States as its national symbol. The image of a bald eagle first appeared on a document signed by George Washington after the Revolutionary War. Since then, it has appeared on coins, stamps, pins, and stationery. While their image became widespread, the birds themselves became harder and harder to find.

In 1969, only a few thousand bald eagles were left in the lower forty-eight states, and the U.S. government added them to the endangered species list. Many thought our national symbol would soon be extinct. What had happened?

Many bald eagles were killed in the first half of this century by ranchers, who considered the birds a threat to their calves and sheep. In Alaska and elsewhere, a pair of bald eagle feet sold for fifty cents, and more than a hundred thousand birds were killed. Although strict laws were passed that made the killing of eagles illegal, the birds continued to disappear.

Eventually, scientists discovered that bald eagles were being poisoned. A deadly pesticide, DDT, drained from farmers' fields into waterways, where it contaminated aquatic plants and small animals. Fish feeding on this aquatic life collected the pesticide in their bodies. Eagles feeding on the fish were then contaminated. After years of being part of this poisoned food chain, many eagles were unable to reproduce. The shells of their eggs were so thin, they cracked before the young were ready to hatch.

The United States banned the use of DDT in 1972, and a captive-breeding program for bald eagles began a few years later. Eagles were hatched and raised in captivity the way captive California condors are being bred now in California. Dozens and dozens of bald eagles have since been released into the wild. As a result of these and other efforts, bald eagles can now be found in every state except Hawaii. They are especially numerous in Alaska, along coastlines, and around the Great Lakes and Chesapeake Bay.

Majestic and powerful golden eagles also live in North America. These birds are covered with dark brown feathers, except for the gold-colored feathers on

A BALD EAGLE'S WHITE FEATHERS BLEND WITH THE SNOW IN ALASKA.

A GOLDEN EAGLE IN
A PINE TREE

the head and nape, for which they are named and the faint white bands across the tail. Feathers cover both legs. You will find golden eagles soaring above the hills, mountains, and canyons of Washington, Oregon, Colorado, and other western states. They are rare in the East. Some golden eagles migrate to Mexico for the winter.

Bald eagles eat mostly fish, but they and golden eagles also feed on herons, ducks, rabbits, and skunks. When pursuing a duck or a goose, the stronger and faster eagle often sweeps beneath it and, turning on its back, thrusts its talons into the prey's breast. The strike of an eagle's powerful feet usually kills rabbits and other prey instantly. After a large meal, an eagle may not eat again for a day or two. Fur, feathers, bones, and other indigestible parts are *cast,* or regurgitated, in large pellets.

When fishing, bald eagles dip their inch-and-a-half-long (4-cm-long) talons into the water and, usually without getting their feathers wet, snag fish swimming close to the surface. Bald eagles occasionally steal food from other birds. With talons extended, an eagle will swoop down on a gull or an osprey flying by with a fish. The eagle rarely strikes the smaller bird, but the swooping action usually frightens it enough that it drops the fish. The eagle then retrieves it, often in midair.

**A BALD EAGLE COMES IN TO SNAG A FISH NEAR THE SURFACE OF THE WATER.**

Hunting requires fancy flying, but eagles perform their best aerial acrobatics during the breeding season. In one courtship display, called *whirling*, exhibited by both golden and bald eagles, pairs lock talons and cartwheel through the air for several hundred feet.

Nesting pairs call loudly at the borders of their territory and will attack intruding eagles. In winter, the birds are far less territorial; they gather in open areas near unfrozen waterways to share major food sources. Some wintering grounds attract both bald and golden eagles.

Like many birds of prey, eagles mate for life. However, if one partner dies, the survivor seeks another. Eagle pairs build a nest of sticks—about 6 feet (2 m) across—in the top of a tree or on a cliff shelf. Breeding pairs will return to the same nest and add new material year after year, often until the huge and heavy nest breaks its supporting limbs.

Usually two eggs are laid on the moss, weeds, grass, and feathers that line the nest. Incubation lasts about thirty-five days and is shared by both bald eagle parents; among golden eagles, only the female sits on the eggs.

By the time an eagle is seven weeks old, its white *down* coat has been replaced with dark flight feathers, and it is jumping, stretching, and exercising its wings. At about eleven weeks of age, the eagle fledges, but it will continue to sleep in the nest at night and eat food caught by its parents for several more weeks. Both bald and golden eagles develop adult plumage when they are four or five years old. By that time, they are ready to choose a mate and build their own nest, which they often do within 100 miles (160 km) of where they were raised.

You are more likely to see bald eagles in the wild now than in recent years past. But even if you just see one on a quarter or a stamp, take a good look and remember how close these birds came to extinction.

# CHAPTER FOUR

## KITES

### GRACEFUL GLIDERS

A large, dark bird flies low along the marshy shore of Lake Okeechobee in southern Florida. It moves slowly in a zigzag pattern, lazily flapping its broad wings. In search of something, the bird looks hard at the shallow water.

The bird, a snail kite, eats only marsh snails. Spotting one, the kite drops quickly, grabs the snail in its talons, and carries it to a nearby perch. The kite pulls the snail from its shell with its long, hooked bill and swallows it whole. The empty shell falls to the ground among hundreds of others.

The snail kite's limited diet is matched by its limited range. You'll find snail kites only around Lake Okeechobee and a few marshy areas in southern Florida, and even here they are uncommon—but not as uncommon as they used to be. It is estimated that in 1965 only about fifty snail kites remained in the area. Today, approximately six hundred snail kites live in Florida.

The hook-billed kite, a gray bird with a striped breast, also lives within a small range—the swamps and woods of south Texas. It, too, eats snails. But unlike the snail kite, it eats many kinds of snails as well as frogs and insects.

With a wingspan the length of a bathtub, the swallow-tailed kite is the largest of the kites. It has a long, forked tail that enables it to turn quickly and stop suddenly. Its striking black and white plumage makes it easy to spot near streams and marshes in the southern United States.

You can identify the Mississippi kite by its fiery red eyes and red-tipped black primary feathers. It has the largest range of all the kites; you can see it along lakes and rivers from South Carolina and Georgia west to New Mexico and Colorado and as far north as Illinois.

Our only west coast kite, the black-shouldered kite, lives in the fields and foothills of Oregon, California, and Texas. The best way to recognize it is to spot its black shoulder feathers, which stand out against the rest of its white and pale gray plumage. Also, you can look for its yellow eyes, legs, and feet.

All five North American kite species have long legs and slender bodies. Propelled by slow and easy wing-beats, they gracefully glide through the air. Except for snail kites, they all eat insects. Able to spot an insect hundreds of feet away, a kite will race to it and grab it in midair with its sharp talons.

A SWALLOW-TAILED KITE GRACEFULLY GLIDING HIGH ABOVE THE WATER.

**EVEN VERY YOUNG MISSISSIPPI KITES
SUCH AS THESE HAVE FIERY RED EYES.**

Kites are more sociable than other birds of prey. After a day of hunting on their own, snail kites gather in groups to roost. Mississippi and swallow-tailed kites sometimes fly and feed together during the day, and you may see them migrating together in large flocks.

Kites build their nests from sticks and leaves in trees that are close to water. If trees are unavailable, black-shouldered kites will nest on cliff ledges, in shrubs, or even on the ground. Usually the male and female work together to construct the nest, but among snail kites, the male builds the nest alone. Females are larger than males among other birds of prey, but female and male kites are nearly the same size. Both sexes, among all species, share the jobs of incubation and protecting and feeding the young.

Month-old kites look similar to their parents, except for streaking on the head, breasts, and under–wings. Kites that survive their first winter will be ready to breed by spring. Snail kites and black-shouldered kites stay in North America year round, while hook-billed kites, swallow-tailed kites, and Mississippi kites winter in Central and South America.

The draining of wetlands and the cutting of forests in Central and South America threaten these three migratory species, who return north each year to breed in fewer and fewer numbers. Additional kite habitat is lost when our own marshes and swamps are destroyed.

That's what happened in the 1950s and 1960s, when thousands of acres of wetlands were drained and developed in southern Florida. This led to the disappearance of marsh snails and in turn of snail kites. But the snail kites hung on. Despite their fragile habitat and specialized diet, snail kites are slowly but steadily increasing in number.

# CHAPTER FIVE

## HAWKS

### BEASTLY BEAUTIES

Imagine yourself running full speed through the woods, dodging trees and jumping over fallen branches. Dark leaves block your view, and tangled vines cover your path. Speeding along, you duck and swerve to avoid collisions. Flying through such a maze is just what some hawks do when they hunt.

These low-flying hawks, superbly adapted for forest cruising, are called *accipiters.* An accipiter's short, rounded wings turn quickly, and its long tail steers with split-second precision. There are three species of accipiters in North America—the northern goshawk, the Cooper's hawk, and the sharp-shinned hawk. Spotting them can be difficult because their dark backs and streaked underparts blend into their woodsy environment.

Another group of hawks, called *buteos,* have broad wings and short tails. Buteos, such as red-tailed hawks and red-shouldered hawks, are easy to see because they spend much of their time soaring and perching in open areas.

Besides accipiters and buteos, two other kinds of hawks live in North America. The northern harrier, formerly called the marsh hawk, flies low to the ground searching for mice, rats, frogs, and other prey. The osprey, also known as the fish hawk, lives near water because it feeds mostly on fish.

Identifying hawks can be difficult because many of them look alike, but most hawks have at least one major identifying feature. Can you guess what it might be on the red-tailed hawk? The red-shouldered hawk? What about the gray hawk, the white-tailed hawk, the short-tailed hawk, and the common black-hawk?

Other hawk names do not reveal characteristics quite so clearly. The zone-tailed hawk, for example, is named for the white bands on its black tail; the rough-legged hawk gets its name from its feathered legs; and the sharp-shinned hawk is named for its unfeathered lower legs. Its wings, large in relation to its body size, give the broad-winged hawk its name, and the name of the ferruginous hawk comes from the Latin word for rust, *ferrugo,* which describes the bird's reddish-brown plumage.

Like other raptors, hawks start their day by stretching, casting, and defecating. They also preen their feathers. After these preparations, the birds leave their roost or nest site and begin to hunt.

AN OSPREY FEEDS ON A FISH, WHICH
IS ITS MAIN SOURCE OF FOOD.

**RANGES FOR HAWK SPECIES**

| Species | Spring/Summer | Fall/Winter |
| --- | --- | --- |
| Sharp-shinned Hawk | Alaska, Canada, mountainous areas of the continental United States, Mexico | continental United States, Mexico |
| Cooper's Hawk | southern Canada, continental United States, Mexico | continental United States, Mexico |
| Northern Goshawk | Alaska, Canada, western United States, Mexico | Alaska, Canada, western, central, and northern United States, Mexico |
| Red-shouldered Hawk *(pictured above)* | southeastern Canada, eastern and central United States, California, Mexico | eastern and central United States, California, Mexico |

| Broad-winged Hawk | Canada, eastern United States | southern Florida, southern California |
| Gray Hawk | Arizona, New Mexico, Texas | South America only |
| Red-tailed Hawk | Alaska, Canada, continental United States, Mexico | continental United States, Mexico |
| Swainson's Hawk | western Canada, western United States, Mexico | southern Florida |
| Short-tailed Hawk | central and southern Florida | southern Florida |
| Rough-legged Hawk | Alaska, northern Canada | most of continental United States |
| Ferruginous Hawk | southwestern Canada, western United States | western United States, northern Mexico |
| White-tailed Hawk | southern Texas, Mexico | same |
| Common Black-Hawk | Texas, New Mexico, Arizona, Utah, Mexico | Mexico |
| Harris' Hawk | Texas, New Mexico, Arizona, Mexico | same |
| Zone-tailed Hawk | Texas, New Mexico, Arizona, California, Mexico | Mexico |
| Northern Harrier | Alaska, Canada, most of continental United States | southern United States, Mexico |
| Osprey | Alaska, Canada, coastal United States | southern United States, Mexico |

**A FERRUGINOUS HAWK FEEDING ITS YOUNG.**

And what excellent hunters they are! There is probably no animal smaller than a rabbit that some kind of hawk will not attack. Accipiters chase their victims; buteos tend to swoop down upon theirs. Although most hawks eat just about any animal, a few have their own specialties. Sharp-shinned hawks, for example, prefer small birds; ferruginous hawks eat mostly jackrabbits; and Swainson's hawks eat insects—as many as a hundred grasshoppers in one day! Ospreys feed on fish that swim close to the surface of the water. Sometimes an osprey in pursuit of an especially large fish is dragged underwater and, on rare occasions, even drowns. All hawks use their talons to kill, and if they finish a meal with their crop bulging, they may not hunt again for a day or two.

The courtship displays of hawks vary as much as their diets—goshawks swoop, ospreys dive and hover, red-shouldered hawks and harriers sail upside down, red-tails scream and dive, broad-wings whistle and soar.

Pairs of hawks often build their large stick nest on a rock ledge or a sturdy tree branch. Ospreys, however, will build their nests on top of utility poles or billboards. And harriers prefer low, wet spots.

Female hawks incubate their two to four eggs for about one month. Once hatched, the nestlings are attentively cared for by both parents—the male provides

**A THREE-DAY-OLD RED-SHOULDERED HAWK SITS BY TWO UNHATCHED EGGS. THE DOWN COAT OF THE NESTLING KEEPS IT WARM.**

most of the food, while the female *broods,* or cares for the young, at the nest.

The young remain in the nest anywhere from four to eight weeks. They spend much of this time hopping about and flapping their wings in preparation for flight. After they fledge, they remain dependent upon their parents for food for several weeks. By fall, the immature birds are as large as their parents, but duller in color. They are fully mature and ready to breed by their second year.

Like other raptors, hawks are sensitive to loss of habitat and to pollution. DDT and metal pollution nearly wiped out the North American osprey population before the pesticide was banned in 1972. The use of DDT in Latin America still threatens hawks, as it does kites and other migratory raptors.

As the sun sets at the end of a day, hawks everywhere return to their roost. To harriers, this means a protected patch of ground, but to most hawks it means retreating to a favorite tree, cliff, or other elevated perch. Some hawks, such as broad-wings, roost in groups. Others spend the night alone or, if it is breeding season, near their mate and offspring. With their head buried in feathers behind a wing, one leg gripping the perch and the other tucked up under their bodies, the birds sleep until morning.

# CHAPTER SIX

## FALCONS

### SKYDIVERS WITH SIDEBURNS

One day in July, 1987, five peregrine falcon chicks were placed in a box on the roof of a twenty-story building in Albany, New York. For ten days, they ate food that was dropped through a hole in the back of the box. The birds never saw the people who fed them; their survival would soon depend on their ability to feed themselves.

While in the box, the birds shed the last of their down coats and sprouted flight feathers. They started to get restless. Then, when they were six weeks old, the door to their box was opened.

Observers watched the birds through binoculars from a nearby building, and people on the ground were ready to help should the birds fall. But the birds could fly perfectly well, and soon they were preying on pigeons, starlings, and sparrows that lived nearby.

More than two thousand peregrines have been bred in captivity and released in the wild since 1974. The species, once extinct in the United States because of DDT poisoning, now can be found in many rural areas as well as in the cities of Baltimore, Chicago, Detroit, and New York.

These birds are amazing in many ways. Not only can they see at a half mile (800 m) what people can see at 30 feet (9 m), but peregrines are among the fastest birds in the world. When hunting, they dive, or *stoop*, at speeds up to 200 mph (322 km/h). Pressing their wings close to their bodies, the birds thrust their heads forward and hurl themselves headfirst toward earth. Transparent eyelids cover their eyes from the onslaught of wind. After knocking prey to the ground with their clenched feet, the peregrine uses its notched bill to sever the victim's spine.

Crested caracaras are in the falcon family, but they are more like vultures in their eating habits and appearance. If you're lucky, you might see one of these long-legged, red-faced birds walking along the ground in Arizona, Texas, or Florida. Their habitat—grasslands and shrub—is disappearing, and so are they.

Another rare species is the aplomado falcon, a gray, white, and cinnamon-colored falcon that once roamed the deserts and grasslands of Arizona, New Mexico, and Texas. Another victim of DDT poisoning, this species may be making a comeback. A few captive-bred aplomado falcons have been released in southern Texas.

ANNE CANEVARI GREEN

**AN AMERICAN KESTREL**

At 10 inches (25 cm) long, the American kestrel is the smallest North American falcon. Its reddish and blue feathers also make it the most colorful. American kestrels can be found in big cities, small towns, rural areas, deserts, woods, and prairies from Alaska and northern Canada to the tip of South America and from California to New York. The birds are populous because they adapt to many different habitats, and they prey upon a wide variety of animals.

The largest falcon in North America, the gyrfalcon (pronounced *jur-ful-cun*), is twice the length of the American kestrel. Gyrfalcons prey upon lemmings, rabbits, and other mammals as well as large birds, such as grouse and ptarmigans. Gyrfalcons live year round in northernmost North America, along the river valleys and mountainous Arctic coast from Alaska to Greenland. They leave this chilly habitat only during rare winters when prey is scarce. Gyrfalcons vary in color according to where they live. They are white in the eastern portion of their range, gray in the central portion, and dark brown in the western portion.

**UNLIKE MOST RAPTORS, GYRFALCONS OFTEN DON'T MIGRATE SOUTH IN THE WINTER.**

The merlin, a heavily streaked falcon, lives throughout Canada and the northwestern states in the spring and summer and migrates to the southern states in the fall and winter. Watch for them flying low just above the ground or treetops pursuing small birds.

Both merlins and prairie falcons supplement their bird diets with bats, mice, lizards, snakes, spiders, and caterpillars. You can identify prairie falcons by a triangular patch of dark feathers in their underwings. These birds live in the dry, open country of the west, from southern Canada to Mexico.

Falcons engage in a variety of courtship displays, from simply strutting along cliff shelves and soaring in circles over their breeding areas to plunging hundreds of feet down the side of a cliff and somersaulting through the air. During courtship, pairs often hunt together. Afterward, they may perch for hours near their nest site, preening and softly calling to each other.

Like vultures, falcons do not build nests. Many use the abandoned stick nests of crows and hawks. Merlins will rake their feet in dirt to form a slight depression known as a *scrape*. There on the ground, well hidden under bushes, they lay their eggs. Peregrines,

*RIGHT: A PRAIRIE FALCON*
*OVER: A FEMALE PEREGRINE*
*FALCON GUARDS HER EGGS.*

gyrfalcons, and prairie falcons make scrapes on cliff ledges. Several captive-bred peregrines nest on the hard ledges of tall office buildings where they were first released. American kestrels favor more sheltered sites and often nest in tree holes, in small openings in the roofs of barns and other buildings, and even in homemade nest boxes.

Most female falcons lay from two to six eggs. During a month-long incubation period, the male supplies the female with food. After the young hatch, the male continues to supply most of the food, while the female broods at the nest. She shields the young birds from the sun and rain and defends them against intruders. The female also cleans the prey and tears it into small pieces for the young.

The female's brooding duties end in a couple of weeks, when the down coats of the young are replaced by a protective layer of feathers. By this time, the growing birds need more food than one parent can deliver, so the female returns to the sky to hunt. Most young falcons fledge when they are about thirty days old and begin feeding themselves several weeks later. To help prepare them, their parents fly nearby with food in their talons and encourage the young to snatch it from them in midair. By fall when migration begins, they are very capable hunters. Most will acquire full adult plumage and begin breeding when they are two years old.

# CHAPTER SEVEN

## OWLS

## HUNTERS OF THE NIGHT

As the sun sets and other birds of prey are settling down for the night, most owls are readying themselves for the graveyard shift. Their nighttime tools are the same ones used by hawks and other daytime, or *diurnal* raptors: sharp talons, a hooked bill, and an appetite for meat.

These nighttime, or *nocturnal,* predators are further equipped with an enormous pair of ears that in some species extend from the top of the head to the lower jaw. Stiff facial feathers amplify and direct sound waves to the hidden ear openings. Owls' sensitive ears pick up the high-pitched noises made by mice, rats, and other prey.

An owl's exceptional sense of hearing is matched by eyesight strong enough to see in near-total darkness as well as people can see in broad daylight. Its large, forward-facing eyes are fixed in their sockets, but its head can turn three-quarters of the way around.

Owls, themselves, are very hard to hear and see. Their bulky, loose-fitting body feathers and fringed wing feathers enable them to soar in silence. Streaked, barred, and dotted in various combinations of black, brown, gray, white, buff, and rusty red, most owls look like part of a tree.

Owls consume virtually any animal that walks, crawls, swims, or flies; only large mammals seem excluded from their menu. Rodents such as rats, mice, shrews, and squirrels are common targets, but birds, snakes, lizards, and spiders are rarely passed over. A few owls specialize; elf and screech owls, for example, dine mainly on beetles, crickets, and other insects, and barred owls eat mostly smaller owls.

Owls pounce on their victims, using their dagger-like bills to swiftly sever the prey's spine. The talons of great horned owls are sharp enough to pierce bone. Owls rarely capture prey in the air like other raptors, nor do they tear their prey into pieces before eating it. In one or two gulps, an owl swallows its prey whole, later casting indigestible body parts.

In all, nineteen owl species live in North America. They occupy a variety of habitats. Throughout the continent, great horned owls inhabit forests, farmlands, and parks. Burrowing owls live in underground burrows at airports, golf courses, and other open areas of the West and of Florida. The 5-inch (13-cm) elf owl

**RANGES FOR OWL SPECIES**

| Species | Spring/Summer | Fall/Winter |
|---|---|---|
| Common Barn-Owl | most of continental United States, Mexico | same |
| Short-eared Owl | Alaska, Canada, northern and central United States | continental United States, Mexico |
| Long-eared Owl | Canada, northern and central United States | continental United States, Mexico |
| Great Horned Owl | Alaska, Canada, continental United States, Mexico | same |
| Barred Owl *(pictured above)* | Canada, eastern United States, Mexico | same |
| Great Gray Owl | Alaska, Canada, northwestern United States | Alaska, Canada, northern United States |
| Spotted Owl | west coast of United States, Rocky Mountains from Colorado to Mexico | same |

| | | |
|---|---|---|
| Snowy Owl | Greenland, Alaska, northern Canada | Greenland to northern United States |
| Eastern Screech-Owl | southern Canada, eastern and central United States, Mexico | same |
| Western Screech-Owl | west coast of Canada, western United States, Mexico | same |
| Whiskered Screech-Owl | Arizona, Mexico | same |
| Flammulated Owl | southwestern Canada, western United States, Mexico | Mexico |
| Elf Owl | southeastern California to Texas, Mexico | Mexico |
| Ferruginous Pygmy-Owl | Texas, Arizona, Mexico | same |
| Northern Pygmy-Owl | western Canada, western United States, Mexico | same |
| Northern Saw-whet Owl | southeastern Alaska, southern Canada, western and northeastern United States, Mexico | southeastern Alaska, southern Canada, continental United States, Mexico |
| Northern Hawk-Owl | Alaska, Canada | same |
| Boreal Owl | Alaska, Canada, northern United States Rockies | Alaska, Canada, northern United States |
| Burrowing Owl | southern Canada, western United States, southern Florida, Mexico | southwestern United States, southern Florida, Mexico |

**THREE GREAT HORNED OWLS
READY FOR NIGHTTIME HUNTING.**

lives in the deserts of the southwest, and snowy owls are found on the flat, treeless tundra in the arctic regions. If prey is scarce on the tundra in winter, snowy owls move south, sometimes as far as North Carolina. Barn owls are common all over the country.

The availability of prey also affects nesting behavior. Barn owls nest nearly every month of the year when prey is plentiful. But when rodent populations decline, the owls may not nest for months, or even years, at a time. Also, in years when prey is scarce, owls may lay only two or three eggs, while in bountiful years, they may lay ten or more.

Most owls do not engage in the courtship displays so common among other birds of prey. Instead, an owl uses its voice to attract a mate. Screech owl mates sing trilling duets, and courting short-eared owls toot loudly.

Like vultures and falcons, owls exhibit little instinct for nest-building. Most lay their eggs in an abandoned woodpecker nest hole or a natural tree hole. Larger owls may use the old stick nests of hawks and crows, adding nothing but a few scattered bones, feathers, and disgorged pellets of their own. The short-eared, snowy, and northern hawk owls often nest on the ground, and barn owls roost and nest in dark cavities of old, abandoned buildings.

Adult owls fiercely defend their offspring against raccoons, skunks, and other predators. Short-eared and long-eared owls will drop to the ground fluttering and shrieking to detract intruders. Young owls instinctively hiss and flatten themselves if frightened.

Keeping the family fed takes up most of the parents' time and energy. An adult barn owl, for example, may deliver as many as twenty mice an hour to its full nest! Two months after hatching, the young owls are fully grown, able to feed themselves, and ready to fly. The following spring, plumed in the streaks, bars, and dots of their parents, they breed.

Locating owls can be difficult, since most of them sleep during the day. But there are ways to find them. Several times each day, owls cast gray, furry pellets below a favored roosting site, such as a pine tree. These pellets accumulate by the hundreds and often indicate the presence of an owl. Also, look for tree holes that show signs of wear and tear.

Sometimes the only way to detect an owl, particularly in poor light, is by its voice. Listen for the distinctive hiss of barn owls, the bark of spotted owls, and the chirp and chatter of elf owls. Barred owls actually hoot; boreal, northern pygmy, and long-eared

**A SNOWY OWL**

**A YOUNG SCREECH OWL HAVING FALLEN OUT OF ITS NEST DISPLAYS A DEFENSIVE POSTURE.**

owls hoo; great gray owls whoo; burrowing owls coo. Named after its voice, the northern saw-whet owl makes sounds like a saw being sharpened. Master of them all is the great horned owl, whose symphony of hoots, barks, growls, shrieks, and screams may last throughout the night. Although the majority of owls are nocturnal, short-eared owls and snowy owls are diurnal. Several, including great gray owls and northern pygmy-owls, are most active at dawn and dusk.

Locating one owl is difficult enough, but monitoring an entire species is nearly impossible. Consequently, the status of many owls is unknown. However, there is little doubt that the continued loss of wilderness areas hurts owl species. For instance, the clear-cutting of timber in Oregon threatens spotted owls, and prime burrowing owl habitat is being wiped out by the sprawl of Los Angeles. Also in the West, burrowing owls have suffered from the rodent-control programs aimed at poisoning squirrels and prairie dogs. The great gray and elf owls also seem to be on the decline, but the cause is unclear.

Barn owls have disappeared from Missouri, Ohio, and many points farther east, although they are increasing in the North and West. The barred owl remains common in the East, and its range is also expanding in the North and West. Populations of the great horned owl, short- and long-eared owls, and the eastern and western screech owls seem stable.

It takes time and patience to see owls and other birds of prey in the wild. But you do not have to be an expert, nor do you have to travel far to watch raptors. By staying alert, you may see the unexpected—an owl streaking across a tree-lined ball field, a hawk perched at the edge of the woods, or a falcon hunting from the roof of a tall building. Birds of prey are powerful, wild, and free. Watching them will help you appreciate the world you live in.

These men are placing a radio collar on a bald eagle to find out where the bird goes and to learn more about its **habitat**.

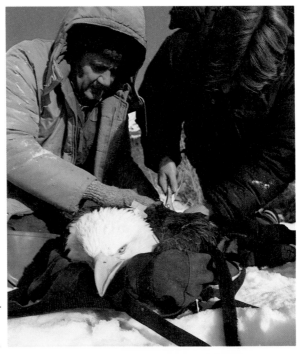

A scientist displays the wing of a peregrine falcon. Falcons have long **wingspans**.

# GLOSSARY

*Accipiter*—a low-flying hawk with short wings and a long tail.

*Brood*—to incubate eggs and cover nestlings.

*Buteo*—a high-soaring hawk with broad wings and a short tail.

*Carrion*—dead animal flesh.

*Cast*—to regurgitate indigestible body parts such as bones and fur.

*Crop*—an enlarged pouch on the side of the throat of many birds.

*Diurnal*—active during the daylight.

*Down*—small, soft feathers that cover nestlings.

*Fledge*—to grow juvenile plumage and take a first flight.

*Habitat*—the place where a plant or animal lives and grows.

*Nestling*—a newly hatched, helpless bird confined to its nest.

*Nocturnal*—active at night.

*Plumage*—all the feathers that cover a bird's body.

*Preen*—to clean, smooth, and rearrange plumage.

*Raptor*—a bird of prey.

*Roost*—to settle down for rest or sleep. Also, the place where birds congregate to rest or sleep.

*Scrape*—a crude nest scraped in the earth by a bird's feet.

*Stoop*—to dive headfirst toward prey.

*Talons*—the long, sharp claws of a bird of prey.

*Whirling*—a courtship display of eagles.

*Wingspan*—the distance between the tips of a bird's extended wings.

# *FURTHER READING*

Alcorn, Gordon Dee. *Owls: An Introduction for the Amateur Naturalist.* New York: Prentice Hall Press, 1986.

Catchpole, Clive. *Birds of Prey that Hunt by Day.* New York: McGraw-Hill, 1977.

George, Jean. *My Side of the Mountain.* New York: Dutton, 1959.

Hogner, Dorothy Childs. *Birds of Prey.* New York: Crowell, 1969.

Lentz, Joan E., and Judith Young. *Birdwatching, A Guide for Beginners.* Santa Barbara, Calif.: Capra Press, 1985.

Maslow, Jonathan Evan. *The Owl Papers.* New York: Dutton, 1983.

National Geographic Society. *Field Guide to the Birds of North America.* Washington, D.C.: National Geographic Society, 1987.

Peterson, Roger Tory. *Peterson's First Guide to Birds.* Boston: Houghton Mifflin, 1986.

Petty, Kate. *Birds of Prey.* New York: Franklin Watts, 1987.

Turner, Ann Warren. *Vultures.* New York: David McKay, 1973.

# INDEX

---

# ABOUT THE AUTHOR

LYNDA DEWITT HAS A MASTER'S DEGREE
IN JOURNALISM FROM AMERICAN UNIVERSITY
IN WASHINGTON, D.C., AND IS AN EDITOR
IN THE EDUCATIONAL MEDIA DIVISION
OF THE NATIONAL GEOGRAPHIC SOCIETY.

SHE HAS WRITTEN SEVERAL ARTICLES ON
BIRDS AND HAS WORKED IN THE FIELD
WITH PEREGRINE FALCONS, SNAIL KITES,
OSPREYS, AND ROYAL TERNS.